Pick Four

Easy Fabric Choices for Great Quilts

Sue Abrey

Martingale®
& COMPANY

Dedication

To all quilters everywhere

Pick Four: Easy Fabric
Choices for Great Quilts
© 2011 by Sue Abrey

That Patchwork Place® is an imprint
of Martingale & Company®.

Martingale & Company
19021 120th Ave. NE, Suite 102
Bothell, WA 98011-9511 USA
www.martingale-pub.com

Printed in China
16 15 14 13 12 11   8 7 6 5 4 3 2 1

Library of Congress Cataloging-in-Publication Data is available upon request.

ISBN: 978-1-60468-020-1

Mission Statement

Dedicated to providing quality products and service to inspire creativity.

Credits

President & CEO ◆ Tom Wierzbicki

Editor in Chief ◆ Mary V. Green

Managing Editor ◆ Tina Cook

Developmental Editor ◆ Karen Costello Soltys

Technical Editor ◆ Nancy Mahoney

Copy Editor ◆ Sheila Chapman Ryan

Design Director ◆ Stan Green

Production Manager ◆ Regina Girard

Illustrator ◆ Laurel Strand

Cover & Text Designer ◆ Regina Girard

Photographer ◆ Brent Kane

Contents

If you don't like scrap quilts, this book is for you! Come to think of it though, if you *do* like scrap quilts, this book is still for you!

During show-and-tell at my quilt group one day, I was showing my latest quilt and realized how often I say, "I can't do scrappy quilts." This led me to think about all the quilts I've made over my quilting years and sure enough, most of them were made with a limited number of fabrics. In almost all of them I had used one, two, or at most three fabrics, plus a neutral or background fabric. That started my brain ticking. Am I the only quilter in the world who's more comfortable with fewer fabrics? I started asking other quilters and found that I wasn't unique. I also became aware that many quilters, no matter how experienced, lack confidence when choosing their fabrics and quilting designs. Thus the idea for this book was born—a book which will help quilters choose fabrics and quilting designs, and most importantly, inspire them to make stunning quilts with a very limited selection of fabrics.

I've divided the book into the following sections:

◆ Guidance on selecting your fabrics, including how and where to look for ideas and color schemes

◆ Techniques for completing your quilt

◆ A section to help you choose quilting designs for your quilts

◆ The projects, starting with those suitable for a beginning quilter or someone looking for a quick project, and finishing with projects for someone who's looking for a challenge

I hope that in this book I can help all you "scrappy-challenged" people out there to believe you can make a beautiful quilt if you just *Pick Four!*

◆ *Choosing Fabrics* ◆

I worked for about three years in a friend's quilt shop, and I've also taught some absolute-beginner classes and various workshops. During these times, the one question that came up more than any other was, "I'm no good with color so how do I choose my fabrics?" I hope that in this section I can show you a relatively simple way of choosing and combining fabrics by using an inspiration fabric, a photo, or even a picture from a magazine.

Find Your Focus

The easiest way to combine your fabrics is to find a medium- to large-scale fabric, such as the ones shown here, that you absolutely love. (If you choose a small pattern, it's still possible to use my method, but it's not quite as easy.)

You may not even use the fabric in your quilt, or you may choose to use it as the backing or just as the binding, but it's going to be your inspiration. Once you have this fabric, which I'll call your focus, you're ready to go.

Find Your Clues

The first thing to remember is that designers usually know what they're doing when they come up with a color scheme for a fabric design, so we're going to use their skills to help us. Looking at the fabric you've chosen, you can decide what the overall color effect is. Is it red, blue, or even "sky-blue-pink" (as my color-blind father always used to name a color if he wasn't sure what it really was)?

A medium- to large-scale fabric becomes the inspiration when choosing colors for your quilt.

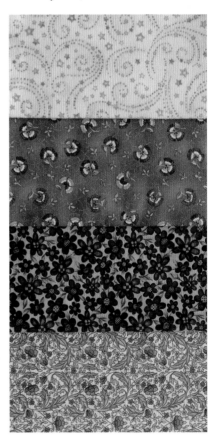

Determine the overall color of your fabric. The first one (top) reads as yellow, the second is green, the next is red, and the last one is blue.

Work Out Your Ratios

It's OK! Come back! Don't panic! We're not going to do any math here. All we're doing now is deciding which color is used most and which least, and so on. This gives you some idea of the color combinations you might want to use. For example, in the fabric below, dark red is the main color, there is some green and a small amount of white, a little lilac, and a tiny amount of yellow. So I might decide that I was going to use the dark red as my main color, green as another, and lilac as an accent with a white background.

The main color in this focus fabric is red.

Choose coordinating fabrics based on the other colors in the focus fabric.

Now Let's Have Fun

Take your focus fabric to a quilt shop (if you aren't already in one) and start looking at the fabrics. With the red fabric I've been using as an example, my first decision has to be whether I plan to use this actual fabric in my quilt. If I'm not going to, then I'd start by finding a similar shade of red, since this is going to be the main color for my quilt. Walk along the fabrics and compare the red in your focus with the red on the bolts. When you find a fabric that is similar and that you like, pull out the bolt. Put your first bolt down on the shop counter or a table. (At this point it would be a good idea to talk to one of the people working in the shop to make sure they don't mind if you take over this way—I don't think you'll be told not to do it.)

Then take the same steps to find the second and third colors. Now you'll want to find some background fabrics that you like and take them to the pile of fabrics. You'll probably get some clues from your focus fabric as to whether the background fabric should be cream, white, tan, or something different altogether. One at a time, lay each background fabric with the other fabrics you've chosen until you find the one you like best.

Now look at the photos below. In each one I've used the same focus fabric, but notice how different your quilt would appear depending on the other colors you choose.

Green and lilac are the supporting colors for the focus fabric.

Change the supporting colors to yellow and copper for an entirely different look.

We've Done It!

Well, almost. Now take your fabrics and unfold a little of each one. Lay them on top of each other, trying to have each one showing in roughly the proportions you will use them in the quilt. Step back a little and take a good look. Do you like what you see? If you do, we're almost there. If not, no problem—you can always start changing fabrics. But in the majority of cases, people are very happy with what they've selected.

One More Thing

Now that you've found your colors, there's one more step to take. You know how everyone always tells us that the fabrics in our quilts should have a variety of scale, from small to large? Have a look at the fabrics you've chosen. Is there some variety of scale? If not, you might want to change one fabric (or more) for a different pattern in the same color, but with a different scale.

Remember, your focus or inspiration doesn't have to be a fabric. It might be a painting that you love, or a photo that you can use in the same way. I have a beautiful photo of my daughter on her wedding day holding her bouquet, and I've often thought that making a quilt with the colors of her flowers would make a lovely memento of her special day.

Your child or grandchild might have a favorite book with an attractively colored cover or a brightly colored toy you could use, if you're planning a quilt for him or her. A picture in a magazine might catch your attention. I've often thought that the pictures in home-interior magazines could suggest good and very up-to-date color schemes.

Wedding bouquet

Fabrics chosen using bouquet colors as inspiration

Here's another color scheme. When he was very young, one of my grandsons had a teddy bear that went everywhere with him.

Blue bear

Fabrics selected using the bear as inspiration

Now think of the famous artist Vincent Van Gogh and his paintings of sunflowers. What colors immediately come to mind? Yellow? Yes, certainly, but there are also browns, greens, and some cream in the painting. Those colors would make a beautiful color scheme for a quilt.

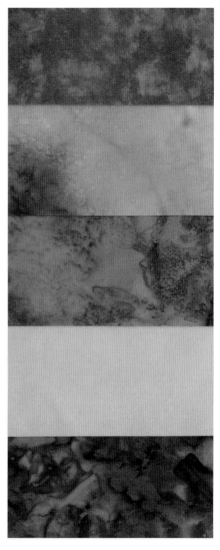

Fabrics chosen based on the colors in a sunflower

An even easier way is to make sure your focus fabric is a quilting-quality fabric, and then choose other fabrics from the same collection. The people who design fabrics for quilting undoubtedly know what they are doing when it comes to color!

Whatever you're using as your inspiration, this method will work. Just remember to take your inspiration with you when you go shopping.

Finally, I want you to remember one thing. There is no such thing as a "right" or a "wrong" fabric in a quilt. If *you* like it, then use it.

This section provides you with all the necessary elements for successfully completing your projects.

Prewashing

I don't generally prewash my fabrics because I like to work with fabrics that feel crisp. If I suspect that a color may run, I'll test it first by putting a small square of the fabric in a glass of cold water and leave it for about an hour. After that amount of time, if the water is colored, I know that I need to wash that fabric before I use it.

Rotary Cutting

The projects in this book are all designed for rotary cutting and are easily pieced by machine. All rotary-cutting measurements include ¼"-wide seam allowances. Basic rotary-cutting tools include a rotary cutter, an 18" x 24" cutting mat, and a 6" x 24" acrylic ruler. You'll be able to make all the projects with these rulers, although I also find a 6" Bias Square® very useful for making cleanup cuts and crosscutting squares from strips.

Cutting Straight Strips

Cutting strips at an exact right angle to the folded edge of your fabric is essential for accuracy. Rotary cutting squares, rectangles, and other shapes begins with cutting accurate strips. Note that the rotary-cutting instructions are written for right-handers; reverse the instructions if you are left-handed.

1. Press the fabric, and then fold it in half with the selvages together. Place the fabric on your cutting mat with the folded edge nearest to your body.

Align the Bias Square ruler with the fold of the fabric and place a 6" x 24" ruler to the left so that the raw edges of the fabric are covered.

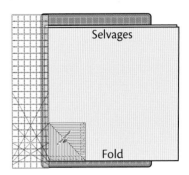

2. Remove the Bias Square and make a rotary cut along the right side of the long ruler. Remove the long ruler and gently remove the waste strip. This is known as a cleanup cut.

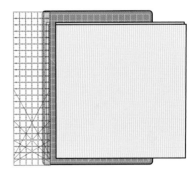

3. To cut strips, align the desired strip-width measurement on the ruler with the cut edge of the fabric and carefully cut the strip. After cutting three or four strips, realign the Bias Square along the fold and make a new cleanup cut.

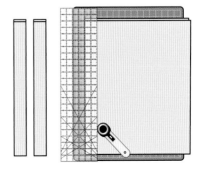

Cutting Squares and Rectangles

To cut squares and rectangles, cut strips in the desired widths. Cut the selvage ends off the strip in the same way that you made the cleanup cut. Align the required measurements on the ruler with the left edge of the strip and cut a square or rectangle. Continue cutting until you have the required number of pieces.

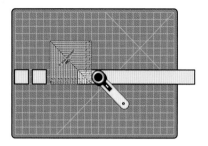

Accurate Seam Allowances

The most important thing to remember about machine piecing is that you need to maintain a consistent ¼"-wide seam allowance. You can test your seam allowance as follows:

Cut two pieces of fabric, 3" x 6", and sew them together along one long edge using a ¼"-wide seam allowance. Open the fabrics, press the seam allowances to one side, and measure your piece. It should measure exactly 5½" x 6". If it doesn't, you'll need to adjust your seam width accordingly. If the finished piece is too narrow, your seam allowance is too wide, so you'll need to make the seam allowance narrower. If your piece measures too big, your seam allowance is too skinny and you'll need to take a slightly wider seam allowance.

Pressing Versus Ironing

Always remember that you're *pressing* the fabrics and seam allowances—not *ironing* them. Press your pieces by holding the iron down on them for a couple of seconds. Then lift the iron and move to the next part. Do *not* slide the iron along the piece; this will only stretch and distort your work.

Making Continuous Strips

1. Using two strips you've cut for your border or binding, place them at right angles, right sides together, and draw a diagonal line across the top strip as shown.

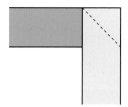

2. Sew along the line and trim the excess fabric, leaving a ¼" seam allowance. Open the fabrics and press the seam allowances open:

3. Repeat with the remaining border (or binding) strips to create one long, continuous strip of fabric.

Adding Borders

None of the quilts in this book have borders with mitered corners, so I've only included instructions for borders with butted corners.

1. Measure the length of your quilt top from top to bottom through the center. Cut two strips from your long strip to this measurement, referring to "Making Continuous Strips" as needed.

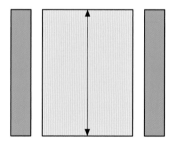

Measure the center of the quilt,
top to bottom.

2. Mark the center of the border strips and the center of the sides of the quilt top. Pin one strip to the side of your quilt, right sides together, matching centers and ends. Ease the quilt top to fit the border strip as you continue pinning the layers together. Repeat with the second strip for the other side border. Sew the side borders in place with a ¼" seam allowance and press the seam allowances toward the border fabric.

3. Measure the width of the quilt top from side to side through the center (including the side borders just added) and cut two strips to this measurement. Repeat step 2 to pin, sew, and press the top and bottom border strips to your quilt top.

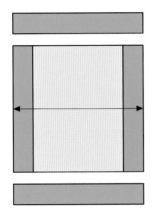

Measure the center of the quilt,
side to side.

Layering and Basting Your Quilt

The batting and backing should be at least 4" to 6" longer and wider than the quilt top. For large quilts, it's usually necessary to sew together two lengths of fabric to make a backing that's large enough. Trim away the selvages before piecing the lengths together and press the seam allowances open to make quilting easier.

1. A day or two before you need your batting, open and lay it flat to breathe. I spread mine over a spare bed; I know some people tumble theirs in a dryer with a damp towel for a few minutes, while others hang their batting on a washing line in a breeze. The choice is yours, but doing this will help eliminate wrinkles and the flattened-down effect from when the batting was packaged.

2. Press your backing fabric and give your top a final pressing.

3. Lay the backing, wrong side facing up, on top of a table or on the floor. (It's great if you can persuade someone to help you with the rest of this process.) Gently smooth the fabric, working from the center out in each direction, until there are no wrinkles. Anchor the edges of the backing with tape or pin them into the carpet to prevent the backing from moving.

4. Center the batting over the backing, lay it down gently, and repeat the smoothing process.

5. Very carefully place your quilt top, right side facing up, over the batting. These three layers together are usually referred to as the quilt sandwich.

You now have to decide how you're going to secure the layers of your quilt sandwich together. If you're going to hand quilt, I would recommend that you thread baste it, but if you're planning to machine quilt, then you'll probably find it easier to use safety pins.

Another option when machine quilting is to use temporary spray adhesive, in which case you'll need to spray each layer as you lay it down, following the manufacturer's instructions. This is very quick, and the layers are repositionable after you have sprayed them. Remember to only use a spray adhesive made specifically for the purpose (your local quilt shop will be able to recommend one), do this in a well-ventilated room (or even better, outdoors), and wash the quilt afterwards if it's a lap or bed quilt.

If you're basting for hand quilting, baste in a grid pattern, about 3" to 4" apart, using large stitches and a thread that contrasts well with the quilt top. If you're planning to machine quilt, use quilters' safety pins and pin in rows, again about 3" to 4" apart.

However, if you plan to have a professional machine quilter quilt your project, check with that person before preparing your finished quilt top in any way. Quilts don't need to be layered and basted for long-arm machine quilting.

Binding Your Quilt

All the bindings in this book have been made with straight grain, double-fold binding. Strips for binding are generally cut 2" to 3" wide, depending on your preference for binding width and your choice of batting. I cut 2½"-wide strips for the quilts in this book. I find it useful to use a walking foot when attaching the binding to the quilt, since I'm sewing through at least four layers of fabric plus the batting. In each project, the cutting instructions indicate how many 2½"-wide strips you'll need to cut for the project.

1. To join the strips into one long continuous strip, sew together strips as instructed in "Making Continuous Strips" on page 10.

2. Trim one end of the binding strips at a 45° angle. Turn under ¼" and press as shown.

3. Fold the strip in half lengthwise, wrong sides together, and press.

4. Trim the batting and backing even with the quilt top using a rotary cutter. Make sure your corners are square and the borders are straight.

5. With the front of the quilt facing up, align the raw edge of the binding with the raw edge of the top, about halfway along one side of the quilt. Leaving 6" at the beginning of the binding (this'll be used to overlap the starting and finishing points) and using a ¼" seam allowance, stitch toward the first corner. Stop ¼" before the corner and backstitch. Cut the threads.

6. Remove the quilt from the sewing machine. Fold the binding straight up and away from the quilt so that the fold forms a 45° angle.

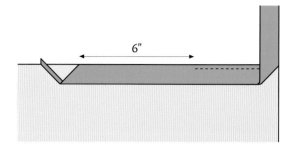

7. Fold the binding back down along the next side of the quilt and stitch to the next corner.

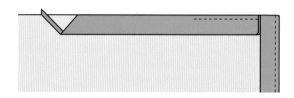

8. Continue around the edge of the quilt in the same manner until you're about 6" from the starting end of the binding. Cut the ending tail 1" longer than needed and tuck it inside the beginning tail. Make sure the binding is flat, and then stitch the rest of the binding. I sew a few extra stitches past the point where I originally started, and then back-stitch.

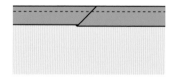

9. Fold the binding to the back of the quilt and slip-stitch in place. With this method, you'll have miters that fall into place nicely at each corner.

"Quilt as desired." That's a phrase to strike terror into our hearts at times, isn't it? I've found that a lot of people really aren't sure just what they *do* desire when they get to the point of quilting their top. In this section, I will help you feel more confident about making your quilting decisions.

Start by spreading out the quilt top somewhere or hanging it where you will see it frequently. My favorite place is to spread it over the settee in my living room where I can keep looking at the quilt top while sitting and reading, watching TV, or sewing down a binding.

Before deciding about the actual quilting designs I'm going to use, I narrow down the choices by asking myself the following questions.

What Type of Quilt Is It?

A wall quilt will probably benefit from a lot more quilting than a bed quilt. This is because a very high density of quilting will make the quilt stiffer, so it will hang nice and straight. A throw for a sofa, on the other hand, might need just minimal quilting so that it's lovely and "snuggly."

How Much Use Will It Get?

If I think the quilt will be washed frequently, such as a baby's floor quilt, I might decide to quilt it a little more than one that will be washed once in a blue moon.

How Much Time Do I Have?

If I want the quilt finished in a hurry, then I'll probably want to do less quilting than if I have unlimited time. If I'm machine quilting it, I find that choosing a simple all-over meander pattern is much quicker than anything else.

Does the Quilt Have a Theme?

This could refer to either the quilt design or the fabric. If I've made a child's quilt top with balloons appliquéd on it, then a quilting design based on clouds might be fun. If my quilt is made with floral fabrics, I might choose to quilt a flower in each block with petals that reach to the corners.

Is the Quilt All Straight Lines or Are There Curves (or the Illusion of Curves)?

Convention says that if your quilt has all straight lines, as in Log Cabin or Nine Patch blocks, then a quilting design with curves is best since it breaks up the angu-larity. Similarly, if your pattern is curved, like Drunk-ard's Path or Dresden Plate blocks, then you might want to use a very regular, straight-line quilting pattern. Although I don't have to stick to these rules (after all, rules are made to be broken, aren't they?) in my experience, there's quite a lot of wisdom in this.

Is There a Lot of "Blank" Space in the Quilt?

By that I mean areas of a single color, which can happen when I place four-patch units together with no sashing to separate them. If so, this might be an ideal place to do some really fancy quilting, since it will show up well.

Are There Any Secondary Patterns?

Sometimes, when I have pieced my top, I find that there's a different secondary pattern standing out. If this is the case, I might decide to emphasize this and obscure the original piecing.

How Are the Borders To Be Quilted?

If there's more than one border, are they to be quilted separately, or am I going to treat them as one border? It's also important to make decisions about any sashing in the quilt. I might decide to use the same design in both the sashing and the borders, or I may want to quilt a different design in each area.

Specific Examples

This long list of questions may seem daunting, but they're the things I take into account when I'm looking at a quilt top. Not all of the questions will be relevant in every case, but they may help you make your decisions.

The same decisions need to be made whether I'm planning to hand or machine quilt and whether I'm going to do it myself or send it out to a long-arm quilter, but remember—what I've tried to explain is just *my* way of making the decisions. With experience, you'll develop your own approaches.

At the end of each project, you'll find a "Quilting Option" section where I explain the quilting decisions that were made for each quilt. Please note that the Munnich Designs (see "Suppliers" on page 78) quilting patterns are copyrighted, are used with permission, and may not be copied without permission from the artist. I hope you enjoy these quilting hints and ideas, and that they help you finish your own quilts.

◆ Double Blue Patches ◆

This is a lovely simple quilt—easy enough for a beginner but pretty enough for anyone who needs a quick project in a hurry, regardless of skill level.

Quilt size: 47½" x 47½"
Block size: 9" x 9"
Skill level: Beginner

Materials

Yardage is based on 42"-wide fabric.

- 1¼ yards of cream tone-on-tone fabric for blocks and border
- 1 yard of dark blue marbled print for sashing and binding
- ⅔ yard of blue print for blocks
- ⅝ yard of yellow marbled print for blocks, sashing squares, and outer-border squares
- 3 yards of fabric for backing
- 52" x 52" piece of batting

Cutting

From the blue print, cut:

- 2 strips, 3½" x 42"; crosscut into 16 squares, 3½" x 3½"
- 7 strips, 2" x 42"

From the yellow marbled print, cut:

- 1 strip, 3½" x 42"; crosscut into 4 squares, 3½" x 3½"
- 7 strips, 2" x 42"
- 1 strip, 1½" x 42"; crosscut into 25 squares, 1½" x 1½"

From the cream tone-on-tone fabric, cut:

- 11 strips, 3½" x 42"; crosscut *6 of the strips* into 64 squares, 3½" x 3½"

From the dark blue marbled print, cut:

- 6 strips, 2½" x 42"
- 10 strips, 1½" x 42"; crosscut into 40 strips, 1½" x 9½"

Making the Four-Patch Units

1. With right sides together, join one blue and one yellow marbled 2"-wide strip along one long edge as shown to make a strip set. Open the strips and press the seam allowances toward the blue strip. Repeat to make seven strip sets. From the strip sets, cut 128 segments, 2" wide.

2"

Make 7 strip sets.
Cut 128 segments.

2. Lay out two segments, rotating one so that the blue and yellow fabrics are opposite each other. Sew the segments together to make a four-patch unit. Press the seam allowances to one side. Trim the unit to measure 3½" square as needed. Repeat to make a total of 64 four-patch units.

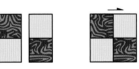

Make 64.

Assembling the Block

1. Lay out four four-patch units, four cream squares, and one blue square in three rows as shown, making sure the blue squares in the four-patch units are positioned in the outer corners.

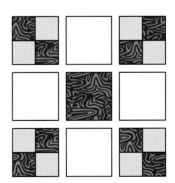

Pieced and quilted by Sue Abrey

2. Sew the pieces together into rows, pressing the seam allowances in the direction shown.

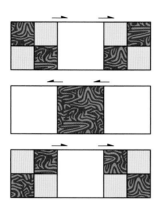

3. Sew the rows together to complete the block. Press the seam allowances toward the center and trim the block to measure 9½" square as needed. Repeat to make a total of 16 blocks.

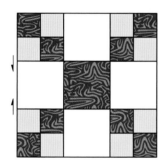

Make 16.

Assembling the Quilt Top

1. Sew together four blocks and five dark blue marbled sashing strips as shown to make a block row. Press the seam allowances toward the sashing strips. Make four block rows.

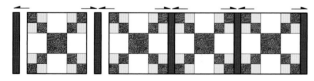

Make 4.

2. Sew a 1½" yellow marbled square to one end of a dark blue marbled strip. Press the seam allowances toward the sashing strips. Make 15 sashing units.

Make 15.

3. Sew 1½" yellow marbled squares to both ends of each remaining dark blue marbled strip. Press the seam allowances toward the sashing strips. Make five of these units.

Make 5.

4. Sew three sashing units from step 2 and one unit from step 3 together as shown to make a sashing row. Repeat to make a total of five rows.

5. Lay out the sashing rows and the block rows, alternating them as shown. Sew the rows together to complete the center of the quilt top. Press the seam allowances toward the sashing rows.

6. Refer to "Making Continuous Strips" on page 10. Sew the five remaining cream strips together end to end to make a long strip. Referring to "Adding Borders" on page 10, measure your quilt top through the center and cut four border strips to this length. Sew border strips to opposite sides of the quilt top and press the seam allowances toward the borders.

7. Sew yellow marbled 3½" squares to both ends of the two remaining border strips, pressing the seam allowances toward the cream strips. Sew the border strips to the top and bottom of the quilt top. Press the seam allowances toward the border.

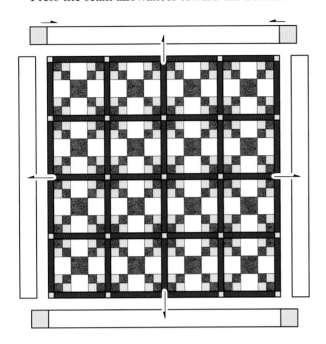

Finishing the Quilt

1. Referring to "Layering and Basting Your Quilt" on page 11, layer the quilt top with batting and backing; baste the layers together. Hand or machine quilt as desired. I used a quilting pattern from Munnich Design. For quilting ideas, refer to "Quilting Option" on page 19.

2. Using the 2½"-wide blue marbled strips, make and attach binding, referring to "Binding Your Quilt" on page 12 as needed.

◆ Color Alternatives ◆

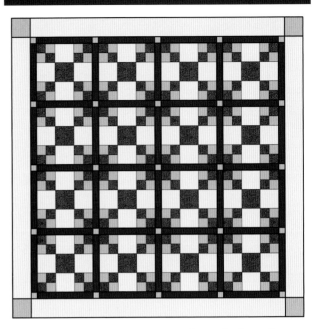

For something soft and pretty, choose dark, medium, and light purples; then pair them with a pink.

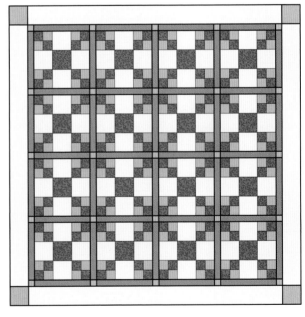

If monochromatic isn't your style, experiment with white, lavender, and green.

This quilt is a throw that will be used fairly regularly. It's a very "square" quilt where all the blocks are made up of squares, the sashing has squares in it, and even the borders have squares in them. It seemed to me that if I quilted a straight-line pattern, it wasn't going to add any contrast to the quilt. So, my decision was easy—I wanted something curvy.

The next thing was to decide if I wanted an all-over pattern or something more intricate. If I was in a hurry, I would have added a curvy allover pattern, but I felt that I wanted something a little more on this quilt. So my second decision was made—I was going to use a custom quilting design.

Then I realized that the sashing was very narrow, so I decided I would quilt motifs that would stretch from the blocks into the sashing; this would join everything and create a secondary pattern. I also thought I would treat the borders separately as a frame for whatever I did in the middle of the quilt. I could've used a small continuous repeat of the block motif in the border, but when I thought about it, I felt it would be too dense in comparison to the center. Another decision made. Now all I had to do was decide on the actual motif and the border design and I was ready to go.

Below you can see examples of two ideas I had for quilting the blocks. The first one was simple straight lines, and the second was a stylized flower extending into the sashing squares.

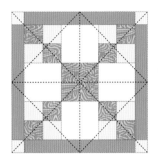 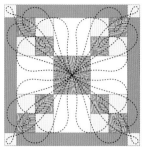

I liked the second idea better, so then all I needed was a border design. The one I chose was a scalloped design, which I felt framed the center of the quilt without detracting from it.

Quilting design copyright is owned by Munnich Design, is used with permission, and may not be copied without the permission of the artist.

◆ Stepping-Stones ◆

"Stepping-Stones" is a deceptively easy quilt to make. It's based on a simple Nine Patch block and is very suitable for a beginner.

Quilt size: 51¾" x 63¼"
Block size: 5¾" x 5¾"
Skill level: Beginner

Materials

Yardage is based on 42"-wide fabric.

- 2 yards of red fabric for blocks, outer border, and binding
- 1⅛ yard of light gold fabric for blocks
- ¾ yard of dark gold fabric for blocks and outer-border squares
- ⅝ yard of green fabric for blocks and inner border
- 3½ yards of fabric for backing
- 56" x 68" piece of batting

Cutting

From the red fabric, cut:
- 5 strips, 5" x 42"
- 4 strips, 4½" x 42"
- 7 strips, 2½" x 42"

From the light gold fabric, cut:
- 8 strips, 4½" x 42"

From the green fabric, cut:
- 2 strips, 4½" x 42"
- 5 strips, 1½" x 42"

From the dark gold fabric, cut:
- 1 strip, 5" x 42"; crosscut into 4 squares, 5" x 5"
- 4 strips, 4½" x 42"

Making Block A

1. With right sides together, join one red and one light gold 4½"-wide strip along one long edge as shown to make a strip set. Open the strips and press the seam allowances toward the red strip.

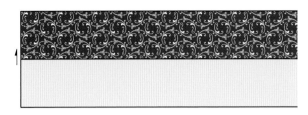

2. In the same manner, sew a second 4½"-wide red strip to the gold side of the strip set from step 1 to complete strip set A. Press the seam allowances toward the red strip. Make two strip sets. From the strip sets, cut 16 A segments, 4½" wide.

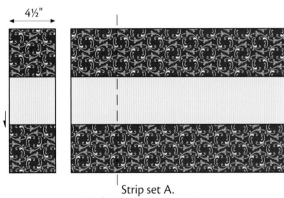

4½"

Strip set A.
Make 2. Cut 16 segments.

3. Repeat steps 1 and 2 using one 4½"-wide green strip and two light gold strips to make strip set B. Press the seam allowances toward the green strip. Make two strip sets and cut them into 16 B segments, 4½" wide. (Set aside eight of the segments for block B.)

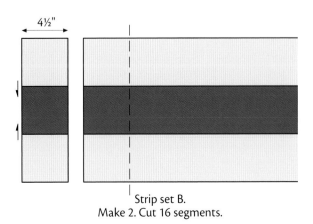

4½"

Strip set B.
Make 2. Cut 16 segments.

Pieced and quilted by Sue Abrey

4. Lay out two A segments and one B segment as shown. Sew the segments together and press the seam allowances in one direction. Make eight nine-patch units.

Make 8.

5. Cut each nine-patch unit in half horizontally and vertically as shown to make four blocks. The blocks should measure 6¼" square. Make 32 of block A.

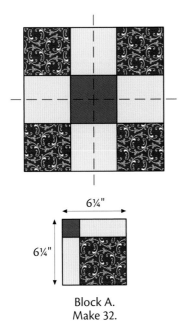

Block A.
Make 32.

Making Block B

1. Repeating steps 1 and 2 of "Making Block A" and using the 4½"-wide dark gold strips and remaining light gold strips, make two of strip set C. Press the seam allowances toward the dark gold strips. From the strip sets, cut 16 C segments, 4½" wide.

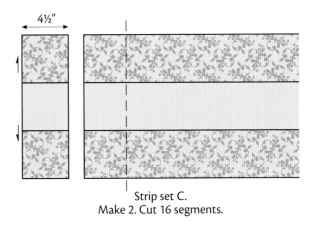

Strip set C.
Make 2. Cut 16 segments.

2. Lay out two C segments and one B segment as shown. Sew the segments together and press the seam allowances in one direction. Make eight nine-patch units.

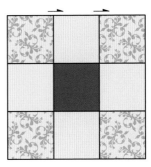

Make 8.

3. Cut each nine-patch unit in half horizontally and vertically as shown to make four blocks. The blocks should measure 6¼" square. Make 32 of block B.

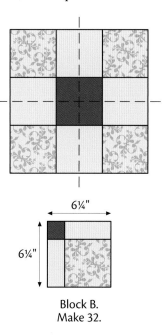

Block B.
Make 32.

Assembling the Quilt Top

1. Lay out the A and B blocks, rotating and alternating them as shown (you'll have one A block left over). Sew the blocks together in rows. Press the seam allowances in opposite directions from row to row. Then sew the rows together and press the seam allowances in one direction.

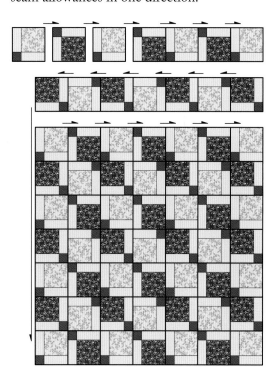

2. Referring to "Making Continuous Strips" on page 10, sew the 1½"-wide green strips end to end to make a long strip. Referring to "Adding Borders" on page 10, measure, cut, and sew the green strips to the quilt top for the inner border. Press the seam allowances toward the border.

3. Sew the 5"-wide red strips end to end to make a long strip. Measure the width of the quilt top through the center and cut two red border strips to this length for the top and bottom borders. Sew dark gold squares to the ends of both strips and press the seam allowances toward the red strips.

4. Measure the length of the quilt top through the center and cut two red border strips to this length. Sew the strips to opposite sides of the quilt top. Press the seam allowances toward outer border.

5. Sew the top and bottom border strips from step 3 to the quilt top. Press the seam allowances toward the outer border.

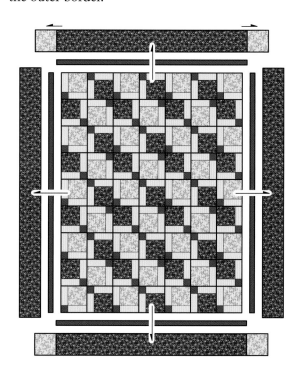

Finishing the Quilt

1. Referring to "Layering and Basting Your Quilt" on page 11, layer the quilt top with batting and backing; baste the layers together. Hand or machine quilt as desired. I used a quilting pattern from Munnich Design. For quilting ideas, refer to "Quilting Option" on page 25.

2. Using the 2½"-wide red strips, make and attach binding, referring to "Binding Your Quilt" on page 12 as needed.

◆ *Color Alternatives* ◆

◆ *Quilting Option* ◆

Since this is a quilt where it's difficult to decide where one block ends and the next starts, the quilt was better suited to an overall pattern, such as the swirly pattern I used. I did consider using a denser pattern, but I really wanted this throw to be soft, so I only did a minimal amount of quilting.

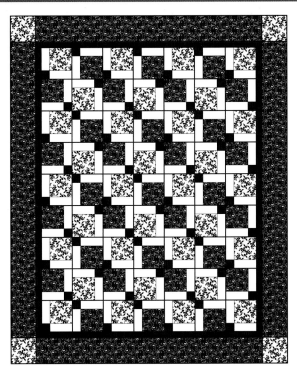

Go graphic with black and white! Choose two black-and-white prints, one dark and one light. Then pair them with a black solid and a white solid.

Quilting design copyright is owned by Munnich Design, is used with permission, and may not be copied without the permission of the artist.

Feeling bright and lively? Why not try some wonderfully modern, bright fabrics in a combination of orange, yellow, and red.

◆ 3-D Noughts and Crosses ◆

With its three-dimensional effect, this quilt may look complicated, but it's actually a very quick and easy quilt that could be made in a weekend.

Quilt size: 80½" x 80½"
Block size: 8" x 8"
Skill level: Beginner

Materials

Yardage is based on 42"-wide fabric.

- 4¼ yards of dark turquoise fabric for blocks and outer border
- 2⅓ yards of light turquoise fabric for blocks
- 1⅓ yards of dark tan fabric for blocks, middle border, and binding
- 1¼ yards of light tan fabric for blocks and inner border
- 5 yards of fabric for backing
- 85" x 85" piece of batting
- Spray starch
- 8½" square ruler or plastic template

Cutting

Since you'll be cutting the squares of dark tan and light tan along the bias edge, I recommend that you apply spray starch to these fabrics and press with a dry iron rather than steam before cutting.

From the dark turquoise fabric, cut:

- 8 strips, 4½" x 42"
- 22 strips, 3⅜" x 42"; crosscut into 64 rectangles, 3⅜" x 12½"
- 9 strips, 2½" x 42"

From the light turquoise fabric, cut:

- 22 strips, 3⅜" x 42"; crosscut into 64 rectangles, 3⅜" x 12½"

From the dark tan fabric, cut:

- 4 strips, 5" x 42"; crosscut into 32 squares, 5" x 5". Cut each square in half diagonally to yield 64 triangles.
- 8 strips, 2½" x 42"

From the light tan fabric, cut:

- 4 strips, 5" x 42"; crosscut into 32 squares, 5" x 5". Cut each square in half diagonally to yield 64 triangles.
- 7 strips, 2½" x 42"

Making the Blocks

The dark turquoise and light turquoise rectangles were cut oversized. After assembling the pieces, you'll carefully trim the block to make it square. This way, you don't have to work with templates or use foundation piecing.

Block A

1. Sew together a light turquoise and a dark turquoise rectangle along one long edge. Press the seam allowances toward the dark rectangle.

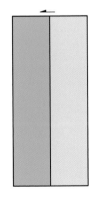

Pieced and quilted by Lis and Drew Moore

2. Fold the rectangle unit in half and mark the center point on the outside edge with a pin. Fold two dark tan triangles in half and mark the center of the long side with a pin. Stitch triangles to opposite sides of the rectangle unit, right sides together and matching the center pins. Press the seam allowances toward the triangles.

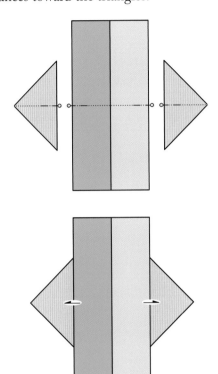

3. Place the block from step 2 on your cutting mat. Center an 8½" square ruler on top of the block, aligning the center seam with the 45° line on the ruler as shown. (The dark tan triangles are slightly oversized, so you should have a small amount of fabric all around the ruler.) Trim the first two sides; then turn the block around and trim the other two sides. The block should measure 8½" square.

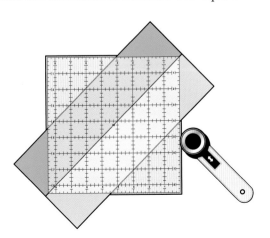

4. Repeat steps 1–3 to make a total of 24 blocks.

Block A.
Make 24.

Block B

Repeat steps 1–3 in "Block A" using dark turquoise rectangles, light turquoise rectangles, dark tan triangles, and light tan triangles to make eight blocks as shown. Make sure you sew the dark tan triangles to the dark turquoise rectangles.

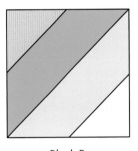

Block B.
Make 8.

Block C

To make block C, sew together two light tan triangles, one dark turquoise rectangle, and one light turquoise rectangle, referring to steps 1–3 of "Block A" as needed. Make 24 of block C.

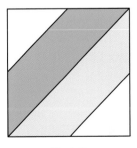

Block C.
Make 24.

Block D

Sew together dark turquoise rectangles, light turquoise rectangles, dark tan triangles, and light tan triangles to make eight of block D as shown. Make sure you sew the dark tan triangles to the light turquoise rectangles.

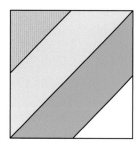

Block D.
Make 8.

Assembling the Quilt Top

1. Lay out the blocks in eight rows of eight blocks each, rotating them as shown below. When you are satisfied with the placement, sew the blocks together in rows and press the seam allowances in opposite directions from row to row.

2. Sew the rows together, matching the seam intersections, and press the seam allowances in one direction.

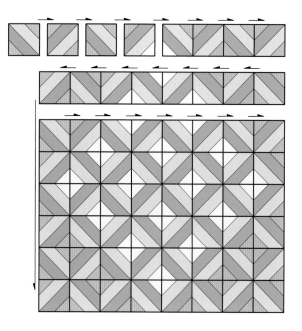

3. Referring to "Making Continuous Strips" on page 10, join the 2½"-wide light tan strips end to end to make a long strip. Referring to "Adding Borders" on page 10, measure, cut, and sew the light tan strips to the quilt top for the inner border. Press the seam allowances toward the border.

4. Repeat step 3 using the 2½"-wide dark tan strips for the middle border and the 4½"-wide dark turquoise strips for the outer border.

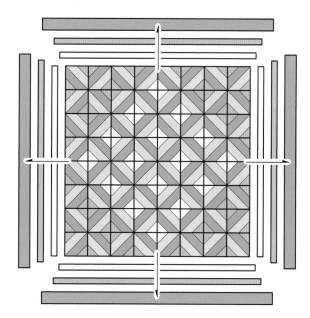

Finishing the Quilt

1. Referring to "Layering and Basting Your Quilt" on page 11, layer the quilt top with batting and backing; baste the layers together. Hand or machine quilt as desired. Lis used a quilting pattern from Munnich Design. For quilting ideas, refer to "Quilting Option" on page 31.

2. Using the 2½"-wide dark turquoise strips, make and attach binding, referring to "Binding Your Quilt" on page 12 as needed.

◆ Color Alternatives ◆

To make this bright green jewel, use a dark green, a light green, yellow, and a creamy beige.

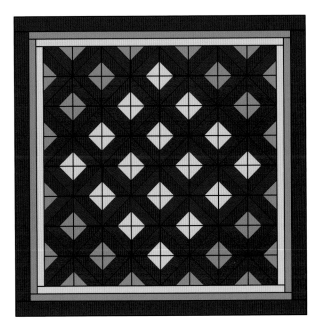

Love chocolate? Then try mixing light, medium, and dark brown with a dash of raspberry for a tasty treat.

◆ Quilting Option ◆

The overall look of this quilt was very angular, so Lis chose to quilt a very curvy, curly motif to soften the look of the blocks. She then used a half motif in the borders to coordinate with the center. Using a half or a quarter of a motif can often be a very successful way of bringing the whole quilt together, especially if you can't find a border pattern that you feel complements the quilting in the center of the quilt.

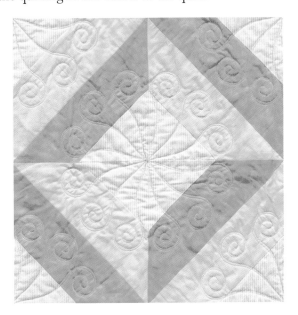

◆ Rickrack ◆

This is a quick, fun quilt to make. You'll start by making large blocks, cutting them into quarters, and then rearranging the smaller blocks to create a zigzag effect. The quilt was named when a friend saw the layout and said it looked like rickrack braid.

Quilt size: 70½" x 88½"
Block size: 9" x 9"
Skill level: Advanced beginner

Materials

Yardage is based on 42"-wide fabric.

- 3⅝ yards of red fabric for blocks and binding
- 3 yards of blue fabric for blocks, border 2, and border 4
- 2 yards of green fabric for blocks, border 1, and border 3
- 5½ yards of fabric for backing
- 75" x 93" piece of batting

Cutting

From the blue fabric, cut:
- 3 strips, 7" x 42"; crosscut into 12 squares, 7" x 7"
- 8 strips, 4½" x 42"
- 5 strips, 3½" x 42"
- 7 strips, 2½" x 42"

From the red fabric, cut:
- 8 strips, 7" x 42"; crosscut into 36 squares, 7" x 7"
- 10 strips, 3½" x 42"
- 9 strips, 2½" x 42"

From the green fabric, cut:
- 3 strips, 7" x 42"; crosscut into 12 squares, 7" x 7"
- 5 strips, 3½" x 42"
- 14 strips, 1½" x 42"

Making the Blocks

The 7" squares for making half-square-triangle units were cut oversized for easier cutting and piecing. After making the half-square-triangle units, you'll trim them to size.

1. Draw a diagonal line from corner to corner on the wrong side of each blue square. Layer the marked blue squares right sides together with red squares and stitch ¼" from each side of the marked line. Cut the squares apart on the drawn line. Press the seam allowances toward the blue triangles and trim each unit to measure 6½" square. Make 24 half-square-triangle units.

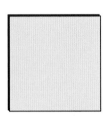
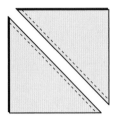

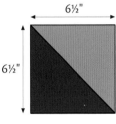

Make 24.

2. With right sides together, join a blue and a red 3½"-wide strip along one long edge as shown to make a strip set. Press the seam allowances toward the blue strip. Repeat to make five strip sets. From the strip sets, cut 24 segments, 7" wide.

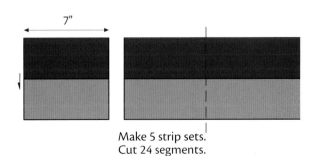

Make 5 strip sets.
Cut 24 segments.

Pieced and quilted by Lis and Drew Moore

3. Lay out four half-square-triangle units from step 1, four segments from step 2, and one 7" red square as shown. Sew the pieces together in rows and press the seam allowances in opposite directions from row to row. Sew the rows together and press the seam allowances toward the center. The block should measure 19" square. Repeat to make a total of six blue/red blocks.

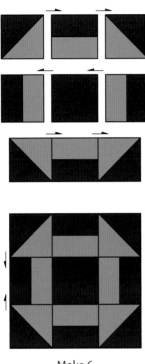

Make 6.

4. Cut each block in half horizontally and vertically as shown to make four smaller blocks. The blocks should measure 9½" square. Make 24.

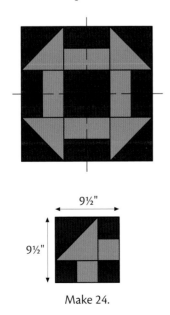

Make 24.

5. Repeat steps 1–4 using the red squares, green squares, 3½"-wide red strips, and 3½"-wide green strips. Make six green/red blocks. Cut each block in half horizontally and vertically as shown to make four smaller blocks. The blocks should measure 9½" square. Make 24.

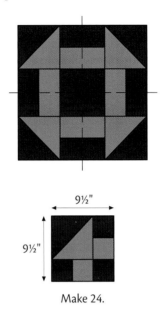

Make 24.

Assembling the Quilt Top

1. Lay out the blocks in eight rows of six blocks each, rotating the blocks as shown. Sew the blocks together into rows and press the seam allowances in opposite directions from row to row. Join the rows and press the seam allowances in one direction.

2. Referring to "Making Continuous Strips" on page 10, sew seven of the 1½"-wide green strips end to end to make a long strip. Referring to "Adding Borders" on page 10, measure, cut, and sew the green strips to the quilt top for the first border. Press all seam allowances toward the border.

3. Repeat step 2 using the 2½"-wide blue strips for border 2, the remaining 1½"-wide green strips for border 3, and the 4½"-wide blue strips for border 4.

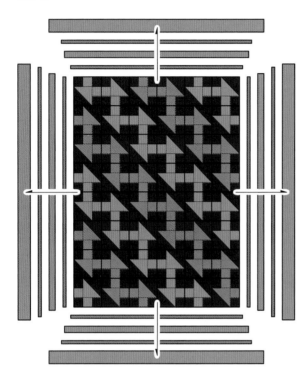

Finishing the Quilt

1. Referring to "Layering and Basting Your Quilt" on page 11, layer the quilt top with batting and backing; baste the layers together. Hand or machine quilt as desired. Lis used a quilting pattern from Munnich Design. For quilting ideas, refer to "Quilting Option" at right.

2. Using the 2½"-wide red strips, make and attach binding, referring to "Binding Your Quilt" on page 12 as needed.

◆ Color Alternative ◆

Increase the contrast by using a white background with medium red and deep maroon.

◆ Quilting Option ◆

It can be quite difficult to choose a quilting pattern for a quilt such as this one, which was made for a young man. Anything flowery or frilly was out of the question. Lis decided to use an allover circular pattern, which successfully added movement and softness to the quilt without being too fussy or feminine.

Quilting design copyright is owned by Munnich Design, is used with permission, and may not be copied without the permission of the artist.

◆ Starstruck ◆

If you love the look of star blocks but hate making half-square-triangle units, this is the quilt for you. The on-point setting makes "Starstruck" unique.

Quilt size: 44¾" x 63"
Block size: 12" x 12"
Skill level: Advanced beginner

Materials

Yardage is based on 42"-wide fabric.

- 2¼ yards of blue fabric for blocks, sashing, border, and binding
- 1¾ yards of light yellow fabric for blocks and setting triangles
- ¾ yard of gold fabric for blocks and sashing square
- 3 yards of fabric for backing
- 49" x 67" piece of batting
- Spray starch

Cutting

Since you'll be cutting the light yellow squares along the bias edge, I recommend that you apply spray starch to the fabric and press with a dry iron rather than steam before cutting.

From the light yellow fabric, cut:

- 3 strips, 3½" x 42"; crosscut into 32 squares, 3½" x 3½"
- 4 strips, 3⅞" x 42"; crosscut into 32 squares, 3⅞" x 3⅞"
- 2 squares, 19¾" x 19¾"; crosscut each square into quarters diagonally to yield 8 setting triangles (2 are extra)
- 2 squares, 11" x 11"; crosscut each square in half diagonally to yield 4 corner triangles

From the gold fabric, cut:

- 6 strips, 3½" x 42"; crosscut into 32 rectangles, 3½" x 6½"
- 1 square, 1½" x 1½"

From the blue fabric, cut:

- 2 strips, 7¼" x 42"; crosscut into 8 squares, 7¼" x 7¼"
- 8 strips, 3½" x 42"; crosscut *3 of the strips* into 32 squares, 3½" x 3½"
- 6 strips, 2½" x 42"
- 9 strips, 1½" x 42"; crosscut *5 of the strips* into:
  2 strips, 1½" x 14½"
  12 strips, 1½" x 12½"

Making the Rectangle Units

1. Draw a diagonal line from corner to corner on the wrong side of each 3½" light yellow and blue square.

2. Place one light yellow square and one blue square, right sides together, on opposite ends of a gold rectangle, making sure the marked lines are parallel to each other as shown. Sew along the drawn line, and then trim away the corner fabric, leaving a ¼" seam allowance. Press the resulting triangles open. Repeat to make a total of 32 rectangle units.

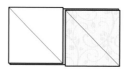 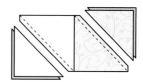

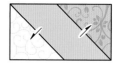

Make 32.

Pieced and quilted by Sue Abrey

Making the Flying-Geese Units

1. Draw a diagonal line from corner to corner on the wrong side of four light yellow 3⅞" squares.

2. With right sides together, place two light yellow squares on opposite corners of a blue 7¼" square and pin in place. The points of the yellow squares will be slightly overlapped and the drawn line should extend across the blue square from corner to corner as shown.

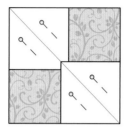

3. Sew ¼" from each side of the drawn line. Cut the square apart on the drawn line. Press the seam allowances toward the light yellow triangles.

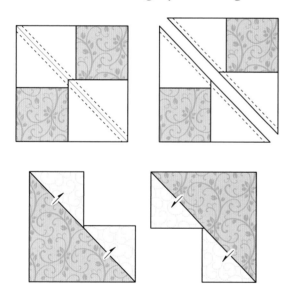

4. With right sides together, place the remaining marked squares on the corners of both pieces. The drawn line should extend from the point of the corner to the point between the two light yellow triangles. Pin in place. Sew ¼" from each side of the drawn line. Cut the pieces apart on the drawn line and press the seam allowances toward the light yellow triangles. You'll have four flying-geese units.

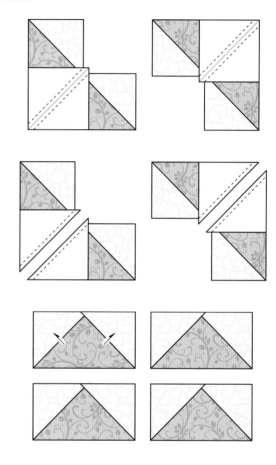

5. Repeat steps 1–4 to make a total of 32 flying-geese units.

Assembling the Blocks

1. Sew a rectangle unit to a flying-geese unit as shown. Press the seam allowances toward the rectangle. Make four of these units.

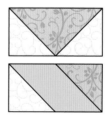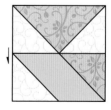

Make 4.

2. Lay out two pairs of units from step 1 as shown and sew them together. Press the seam allowances as shown. Make two half-block units.

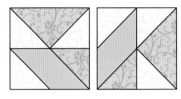

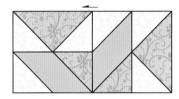

Make 2.

3. Sew two half-block units together to complete the block and press. Repeat steps 1–3 to make a total of eight blocks.

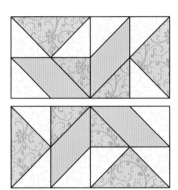

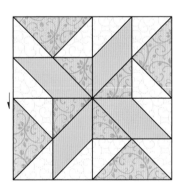

Make 8.

Assembling the Quilt Top

The setting triangles were cut slightly oversized for easier cutting and piecing. You'll trim them after the quilt center is assembled.

1. Lay out three blocks and four 1½" x 12½" blue sashing strips as shown. Sew the pieces together to make a row. Press the seam allowances toward the sashing strips. Make two rows.

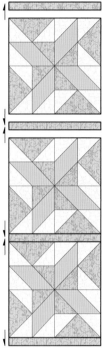

Make 2.

2. Sew 1½" x 12½" blue sashing strips to opposite sides of a block and press the seam allowances toward the sashing strips. Make two.

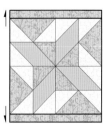

Make 2.

3. Sew a 1½" x 14½" blue sashing strip to one side of each row from step 2. Sew light yellow setting triangles to opposite sides of these rows as shown. Then sew a light yellow corner triangle to the sashing side of each row, making sure the triangles are oriented as shown. Press the seam allowances toward the triangles. Make two.

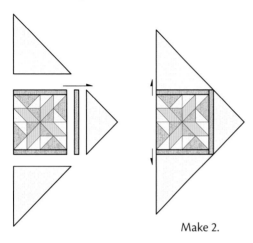

Make 2.

4. Referring to "Making Continuous Strips" on page 10, sew the remaining four 1½"-wide blue strips together end to end to make a long strip. From the strip, cut two 40½"-long strips and two 26½"-long strips.

5. Sew a 40½"-long blue strip to the left side of each row from step 1. Press the seam allowances toward the strip. Sew a light yellow setting triangle to one end of each row, making sure to position the triangle as shown. Press the seam allowances toward the triangle. Make two.

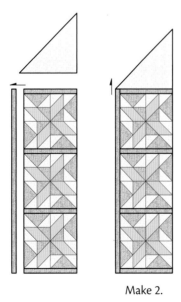

Make 2.

6. Sew the gold square between the two 26½"-long blue strips. Press the seam allowances toward the blue strips.

7. Join the two block rows from step 5 and the blue strip from step 6, rotating one block row as shown. Press the seam allowances toward the blue strip.

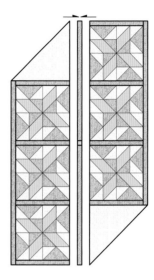

8. Lay out the corner units from step 3, the block rows from step 7, and the two remaining light yellow corner triangles as shown. Sew the pieces together and press the seam allowances as shown. Trim and square up the quilt top, making sure to leave ¼" beyond the points of all the sashing strips for seam allowances.

9. Referring to "Making Continuous Strips" on page 10, sew the 3½"-wide blue strips together end to end to make a long strip. Referring to "Adding Borders" on page 10, measure, cut, and sew the blue strips to the quilt top for the outer border. Press the seam allowances toward the border.

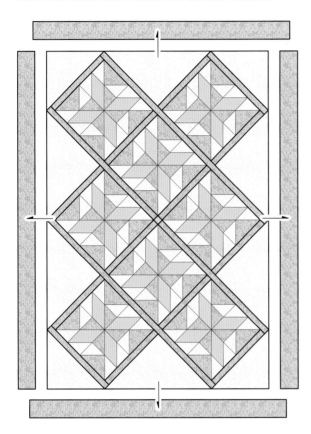

Finishing the Quilt

1. Referring to "Layering and Basting Your Quilt" on page 11, layer the quilt top with batting and backing; baste the layers together. Hand or machine quilt as desired. I used a quilting pattern from Munnich Design. For quilting ideas, refer to "Quilting Option" at right.

2. Using the 2½"-wide blue strips, make and attach binding, referring to "Binding Your Quilt" on page 12 as needed.

◆ Color Alternative ◆

In this version, orange pops against light and medium blues.

◆ Quilting Option ◆

This fun quilt was not intended to be a formal bed quilt, but more a cheerful one that could be dragged out when someone just needed a bit of cheering up, so I chose to just quilt it with oversized loopy circles in each block. I then used half and quarter motifs in the setting triangles. The sashing strips were very narrow, so I chose not to quilt anything in them. Finally, I used a very simple rope design in the border.

◆ Woodland Walk ◆

"Woodland Walk" is a very striking quilt with blocks that are simple to make. Once the blocks are made, there are a number of different layouts you could use for them. On page 45, I've shown three sample layouts to help you choose, but there are many more. Play with the blocks and find your favorite layout.

Quilt size: 74½" x 86½"
Block size: 6" x 6"
Skill level: Intermediate

Materials

Yardage is based on 42"-wide fabric.

- 4⅜ yards of dark green batik for blocks and outer border
- 1½ yards of cream tone-on-tone fabric for blocks
- 1¼ yards of light green batik for blocks
- 1⅛ yards of red tone-on-tone fabric for inner border and binding
- 5⅜ yards of fabric for backing
- 79" x 91" piece of batting
- Spray starch

Cutting

Since you'll be cutting the squares of dark green and cream along the bias edge, I recommend that you apply spray starch to these fabrics and press with a dry iron rather than steam before cutting.

From the cream tone-on-tone fabric, cut:

- 12 strips, 3⅞" x 42"; crosscut into 120 squares, 3⅞" x 3⅞". Cut each square in half diagonally to yield 240 triangles.

From the light green batik, cut:

- 11 strips, 3½" x 42"; crosscut into 120 squares, 3½" x 3½"

From the dark green batik, cut:

- 12 strips, 6⅞" x 42"; crosscut into 60 squares, 6⅞" x 6⅞". Cut each square in half diagonally to yield 120 triangles.
- 9 strips, 6½" x 42"

From the red tone-on-tone fabric, cut:

- 9 strips, 2½" x 42"
- 7 strips, 1½" x 42"

Making the Blocks

1. Sew a cream tone-on-tone triangle to a light green batik square and press the seam allowances toward the triangle. Sew a second cream tone-on-tone triangle to an adjacent side of the square as shown. Press the seam allowances toward the triangles. Make 120.

Make 120.

2. Sew a dark green triangle to each unit from step 1 and press the seam allowances toward the dark green triangles. Trim each block to measure 6½" square as needed. Make 120 blocks.

Make 120.

Assembling the Quilt Top

Once you've made all of the blocks, you'll need to decide on a layout for your quilt. You can choose one of the three layouts shown, or you can play with your blocks to find a layout you like. Keep in mind that for the borders to fit, your layout must be 12 rows of 10 blocks each.

Pieced and quilted by Sue Abrey

1. When you've decided on the layout, sew the blocks together into rows and press the seam allowances in opposite directions from row to row. Then sew the rows together and press the seam allowances in one direction.

2. Referring to "Making Continuous Strips" on page 10, sew the 1½"-wide red strips together end to end to make a long strip. Referring to "Adding Borders" on page 10, measure, cut, and sew the red strips to the quilt top for the inner border. Press the seam allowances toward the border.

3. Sew the 6½"-wide dark green strips together end to end to make a long strip. Measure, cut, and sew the dark green strips to the quilt top for the outer border. Press the seam allowances toward the outer border.

Finishing the Quilt

1. Referring to "Layering and Basting Your Quilt" on page 11, layer the quilt top with batting and backing; baste the layers together. Hand or machine quilt as desired. I used a quilting pattern from Munnich Design. For quilting ideas, refer to "Quilting Option" below.

2. Using the 2½"-wide red strips, make and attach binding, referring to "Binding Your Quilt" on page 12 as needed.

◆ Quilting Option ◆

This quilt has 120 blocks—a quilting motif in each of the 6" blocks would be too busy and the quilting quite dense. The quilt was made from batiks, so I didn't want quilting that would make the quilt stiff. I decided an allover quilting design would be most suitable and since the blocks and overall quilt were very angular, I felt that a curvy pattern would complement it best. I considered several patterns before finally settling on a pattern that suggested pathways to me. Another option would have been to use an allover meandering leaf design, bearing in mind the quilt's name, "Woodland Walk."

◆ Drew's Windmills ◆

*This quilt was named for Drew, whose favorite "quilty"
saying is "Bright red is definitely a neutral."*

Quilt size: 46½" x 52½"
Block size: 6" x 6"
Skill level: Intermediate

Materials

Yardage is based on 42"-wide fabric.

- 2¼ yards of red fabric for blocks and outer border
- 1 yard of blue fabric for blocks and binding
- ½ yard of yellow fabric for blocks and inner border
- ¼ yard of green fabric for blocks
- 3 yards of fabric for backing
- 51" x 57" piece of batting
- Spray starch

Cutting

Since you'll be cutting the squares along the bias edge, I recommend that you apply spray starch to these fabrics and press with a dry iron rather than steam before cutting.

From the red fabric, cut:

- 5 strips, 6⅞" x 42"; crosscut into 21 squares, 6⅞" x 6⅞". Cut each square in half diagonally to yield 42 triangles.
- 5 strips, 4½" x 42"
- 2 strips, 2⅞" x 42"; crosscut into 21 squares, 2⅞" x 2⅞". Cut each square in half diagonally to yield 42 triangles.
- 3 strips, 2½" x 42"; crosscut into 42 squares, 2½" x 2½"

From the blue fabric, cut:

- 12 strips, 2½" x 42"; crosscut *6 of the strips* into 84 squares, 2½" x 2½"

From the green fabric, cut:

- 2 strips, 2⅞" x 42"; crosscut into 21 squares, 2⅞" x 2⅞". Cut each square in half diagonally to yield 42 triangles.

From the yellow fabric, cut:

- 2 strips, 2⅞" x 42"; crosscut into 21 squares, 2⅞" x 2⅞". Cut each square in half diagonally to yield 42 triangles.
- 5 strips, 1½" x 42"

Making the Blocks

1. Lay out one green triangle, one small red triangle, one yellow triangle, two blue squares, and one red square as shown. Sew the pieces together into rows, pressing the seam allowances as shown. Sew the rows together and press. Make 42.

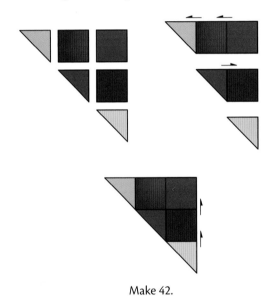

Make 42.

2. Sew a large red triangle to the unit from step 1 and press the seam allowances toward the large red triangle. Trim the block to 6½" square as needed. Make a total of 42 blocks.

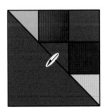

Make 42.

Pieced and quilted by Lis and Drew Moore

Assembling the Quilt Top

1. Lay out the blocks in seven rows of six blocks each, rotating the blocks as shown. Sew the blocks together into rows. Press the seam allowances in opposite directions from row to row. Then sew the rows together and press the seam allowances in one direction.

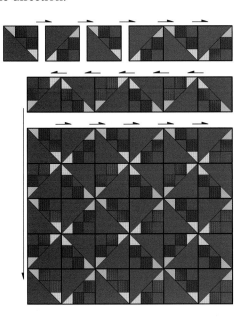

2. Referring to "Making Continuous Strips" on page 10, sew the 1½"-wide yellow strips together end to end to make a long strip. Referring to "Adding Borders" on page 10, measure, cut, and sew the yellow strips to the quilt top for the inner border. Press the seam allowances toward the border.

3. Sew the 4½"-wide red strips together end to end to make a long strip. Measure, cut, and sew the red strips to the quilt top for the outer border. Press the seam allowances toward the outer border.

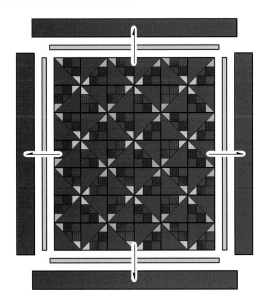

Finishing the Quilt

1. Referring to "Layering and Basting Your Quilt" on page 11, layer the quilt top with batting and backing; baste the layers together. Hand or machine quilt as desired. For quilting ideas, refer to "Quilting Option" below.

2. Using the remaining 2½"-wide blue strips, make and attach binding, referring to "Binding Your Quilt" on page 12 as needed.

◆ Quilting Option ◆

An allover pattern was chosen by Lis to soften the lines of the blocks while at the same time giving a sense of movement to this quilt. It would be very easy to just see the red fabric when looking at the quilt, so using an allover pattern helped move the eye over the entire quilt rather than concentrating on one block or one area. This method is very useful when you want to add interest to your quilt.

◆ Stars at the Crossroads ◆

This quilt is a great opportunity to use a focus fabric in the center of each block. The combination of two different blocks creates a lovely secondary pattern.

Quilt size: 56½" x 72½"
Block size: 8" x 8"
Skill level: Intermediate

Materials

Yardage is based on 42"-wide fabric.

- 2⅛ yards of burgundy fabric for blocks and outer border
- 2 yards of cream fabric for blocks and middle border
- 1⅓ yards of floral fabric for blocks and binding
- ⅞ yard of pink fabric for blocks and inner border
- 3⅝ yards of fabric for backing
- 61" x 77" piece of batting

Cutting

From the cream fabric, cut:
- 3 strips, 5¼" x 42"; crosscut into 18 squares, 5¼" x 5¼"
- 6 strips, 3½" x 42"
- 4 strips, 3" x 42"; crosscut into 34 squares, 3" x 3"
- 5 strips, 2½" x 42"; crosscut into 72 squares, 2½" x 2½"

From the burgundy fabric, cut:
- 7 strips, 4½" x 42"
- 4 strips, 3" x 42"; crosscut into 34 squares, 3" x 3"
- 9 strips, 2½" x 42"; crosscut into 68 rectangles, 2½" x 4½"

From the floral fabric, cut:
- 5 strips, 4½" x 42"; crosscut into 35 squares, 4½" x 4½"
- 7 strips, 2½" x 42"

From the pink fabric, cut:
- 6 strips, 2⅞" x 42"; crosscut into 72 squares, 2⅞" x 2⅞"
- 5 strips, 1½" x 42"

Making the Snowball Blocks

1. Draw a diagonal line from corner to corner on the wrong side of each 3" cream square. Layer the marked cream squares right sides together with the burgundy squares and stitch ¼" from each side of the marked line. Cut the squares apart on the drawn line. Make 68 half-square-triangle units. Press the seam allowances toward the burgundy triangles. Trim each unit to measure 2½" square.

Make 68.

2. Lay out four half-square-triangle units, four burgundy rectangles, and one floral square in three rows as shown. Sew the pieces together into rows and press the seam allowances as shown. Sew the rows together. Press the seam allowances toward the center of the block. Trim the block to 8½" square as needed. Repeat to make a total of 17 Snowball blocks.

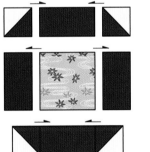
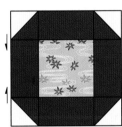

Make 17.

Making the Star Blocks

1. Draw a diagonal line from corner to corner on the wrong side of four pink squares.

2. With right sides together, place two pink squares on opposite corners of a 5¼" cream square and pin in place. The points of the pink squares will be slightly overlapped and the drawn line should extend across the cream square from corner to corner as shown.

Pieced and quilted by Sue Abrey

3. Sew ¼" from each side of the drawn line. Cut the square apart on the drawn line. Press the seam allowances toward the pink triangles.

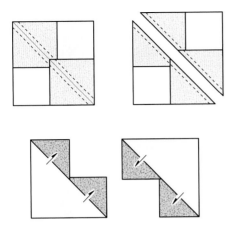

4. With right sides together, place the remaining marked squares on the corners of both pieces. The drawn line should extend from the point of the corner to the point between the two pink triangles. Pin in place. Sew ¼" from each side of the drawn line. Cut the pieces apart on the drawn line and press the seam allowances toward the pink triangles. You'll have four flying-geese units.

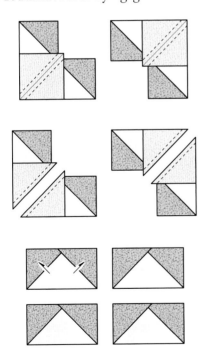

5. Repeat steps 1–4 to make a total of 72 flying-geese units.

6. Lay out four flying-geese units, four 2½" cream squares, and one floral square as shown. Sew the pieces together into rows and press the seam allowances as shown. Sew the rows together, pressing the seam allowances away from the center of the block. Trim the block to 8½" square as needed. Make a total of 18 Star blocks.

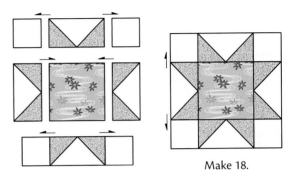

Make 18.

Assembling the Quilt Top

1. Lay out the blocks in seven rows of five blocks each, alternating the blocks as shown. Sew the blocks together into rows and press the seam allowances in opposite directions from row to row. Sew the rows together, pressing the seam allowances in one direction.

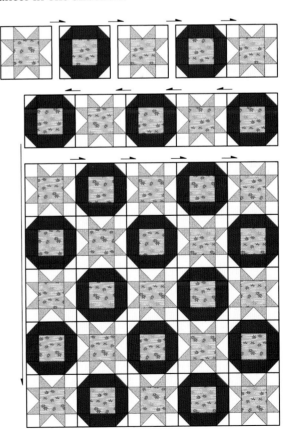

2. Referring to "Making Continuous Strips" on page 10, sew the 1½"-wide pink strips together end to end to make a long strip. Referring to "Adding Borders" on page 10, measure, cut, and sew the pink strips to the quilt top for the inner border. Press the seam allowances toward the border.

3. Repeat step 2 using the 3½"-wide cream strips for the middle border and the 4½"-wide burgundy strips for the outer border.

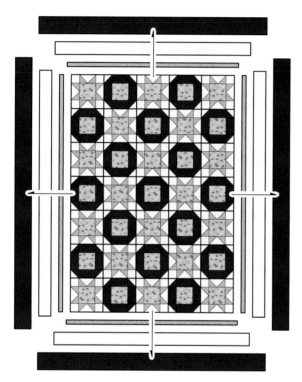

Finishing the Quilt

1. Referring to "Layering and Basting Your Quilt" on page 11, layer the quilt top with batting and backing; baste the layers together. Hand or machine quilt as desired. I used a quilting pattern from Munnich Design. For quilting ideas, refer to "Quilting Option" at right.

2. Using the 2½"-wide floral strips, make and attach binding, referring to "Binding Your Quilt" on page 12 as needed.

◆ Quilting Option ◆

This quilt is made from two separate blocks and my first idea was to use two different quilting designs, but when I thought about it some more, I felt that it was going to be altogether too busy and would detract from the focus fabric in the center of the blocks. I decided to use a four-leaf clover motif in each block, and to make the motif a little smaller than the block. The reason for doing this is that if the motifs were all the same size, they would be touching each other, and that would give the effect of an allover pattern.

Below are the two designs I considered for the blocks. The first diagram shows the two different quilting designs I decided wouldn't work. The other diagram is the four-leaf clover motif I decided to use.

Quilting design copyright is owned by Munnich Design, is used with permission, and may not be copied without the permission of the artist.

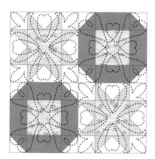 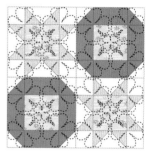

Two quilting motifs   Four-leaf clover motif

My other decision was that I would treat all of the borders as one and chose a feather design for this part of the quilt because I liked the look. In the corners of the borders, I decided to use the same motif as I did in the blocks.

Quilting design copyright is owned by Munnich Design, is used with permission, and may not be copied without the permission of the artist.

◆ Diamonds for Christmas ◆

When it comes to quilts, nothing says "Christmas" to me more than red and gold in a quilt. This is another versatile block that you can use in several layouts—choose your favorite.

Quilt size: 62½" x 78½"
Block size: 8" x 8"
Skill level: Intermediate

Materials

Yardage is based on 42"-wide fabric.

- 4 yards of red fabric for blocks and outer border
- 1⅔ yards of gold fabric for blocks, inner border, and binding
- 1 yard of cream fabric for blocks
- 4⅞ yards of fabric for backing
- 67" x 83" piece of batting
- Spray starch
- 8½" square ruler or plastic template

Cutting

Since you'll be cutting the squares of red and cream along the bias edge, I recommend that you apply spray starch to these fabrics and press with a dry iron rather than steam before cutting.

From the red fabric, cut:

- 6 strips, 9" x 42"; crosscut into 24 squares, 9" x 9". Cut each square in half diagonally to yield 48 triangles.
- 8 strips, 6½" x 42"
- 8 strips, 3" x 42"; crosscut into 96 squares, 3" x 3"

From the gold fabric, cut:

- 8 strips, 3" x 42"; crosscut into 96 squares, 3" x 3"
- 8 strips, 2½" x 42"
- 6 strips, 1½" x 42"

From the cream fabric, cut:

- 6 strips, 4⅞" x 42"; crosscut into 48 squares, 4⅞" x 4⅞". Cut each square in half diagonally to yield 96 triangles.

Making the Blocks

1. Draw a diagonal line from corner to corner on the wrong side of each gold square. Layer the marked gold squares right sides together with the red squares and stitch ¼" from each side of the marked line. Cut the squares apart on the drawn line. Press the seam allowances toward the red triangles. Trim each unit to measure 2½" square. Make 192 half-square-triangle units.

Make 192.

2. Lay out four half-square-triangle units, rotating them as shown. Sew the units together in pairs, and then sew the pairs together to make a pinwheel unit. Press the seam allowances as shown. (Note you may wish to press the last seam allowance open to reduce bulk.) Make 48 pinwheel units.

Make 48.

3. Sew two cream triangles to a pinwheel unit from step 2 as shown. Press the seam allowances toward the cream triangles. Make 48 of these units.

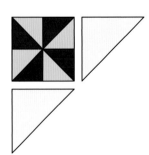 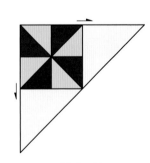

Make 48.

Pieced and quilted by Lis and Drew Moore

4. Layer a triangle unit from step 3 right sides together with a red triangle. With the pieced triangle on top so that you can see the seam intersections, sew the triangles together. Press the seam allowances toward the red triangle. The red triangle is slightly oversized and will be trimmed in the next step.

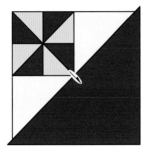

5. Place the block from step 4 on your cutting mat. Place an 8½" square ruler on top of the block, aligning the center seam with the 45° line on the ruler as shown. Trim the first two sides; then turn the block around and trim the other two sides as needed. The block should measure 8½" square.

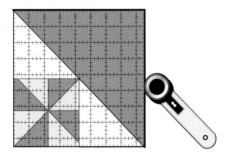

6. Repeat steps 4 and 5 to make a total of 48 blocks.

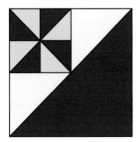

Make 48.

Assembling the Quilt Top

Once you've made all of the blocks, you'll need to decide on a layout for your quilt. You can choose one of the three layouts shown, or you can play with your blocks to find a layout you like. Keep in mind that for the borders to fit, your layout must be eight rows of six blocks each.

1. When you've decided on your layout, sew the blocks together into rows and press the seam allowances in opposite directions from row to row. Then sew the rows together and press the seam allowances in one direction.

2. Referring to "Making Continuous Strips" on page 10, sew the 1½"-wide gold strips together end to end to make a long strip. Referring to "Adding Borders" on page 10, measure, cut, and sew the gold strips to the quilt top for the inner border. Press the seam allowances toward the border.

3. Sew the 6½"-wide red strips together end to end to make a long strip. Then measure, cut, and sew the red strips to the quilt top for the outer border. Press the seam allowances toward the outer border.

Finishing the Quilt

1. Referring to "Layering and Basting Your Quilt" on page 11, layer the quilt top with batting and backing; baste the layers together. Hand or machine quilt as desired. Lis used a quilting pattern from Munnich Design. For quilting ideas, refer to "Quilting Option" at right.

2. Using the 2½"-wide gold strips, make and attach binding, referring to "Binding Your Quilt" on page 12 as needed.

◆ Color Alternative ◆

What a difference color makes! Try teal, orange, and white for a quilt with a different feel.

◆ Quilting Option ◆

Lis chose to quilt a gorgeous feather motif in each block. Why? Because she loves feather designs, and the soft swirls look nice with the pinwheels in the quilt blocks.

Quilting design copyright is owned by Munnich Design, is used with permission, and may not be copied without the permission of the artist.

◆ Poppy Twist ◆

I love this quilt for its drama, which is created from the fabrics I used. I also love the secondary pattern that appears when four blocks are sewn together.

Quilt size: 48½" x 57½"
Block size: 9" x 9"
Skill level: Advanced

Materials

Yardage is based on 42"-wide fabric.

- 2¼ yards of red floral for blocks and outer border
- 1½ yards of black print for blocks, inner border, and binding
- ¾ yard of cream fabric for blocks
- 3 yards of fabric for backing
- 53" x 62" piece of batting
- Spray starch

Cutting

Since you'll be cutting the squares along the bias edge, I recommend that you apply spray starch to the fabrics and press with a dry iron rather than steam before cutting.

From the red floral, cut:

- 4 strips, 5¾" x 42"; crosscut into 20 squares, 5¾" x 5¾". Cut each square diagonally into quarters to yield 80 triangles.
- 5 strips, 5½" x 42"
- 3 strips, 5" x 42"; crosscut into 20 squares, 5" x 5"

From the black print, cut:

- 4 strips, 5¾" x 42"; crosscut into 20 squares, 5¾" x 5¾". Cut each square diagonally into quarters to yield 80 triangles.
- 6 strips, 2½" x 42"
- 5 strips, 1½" x 42"

From the cream fabric, cut:

- 4 strips, 5¾" x 42"; crosscut into 20 squares, 5¾" x 5¾". Cut each square diagonally into quarters to yield 80 triangles.

Making the Blocks

1. Fold a 5" red floral square in half and mark the center on opposite sides with pins. Fold two black triangles in half and mark the centers of the long side with pins. Matching the center pins and with right sides together, sew the triangles to opposite sides of the red square. Press the seam allowances toward the black triangles.

2. In the same manner, center and sew black triangles to the remaining two sides of the red square. Press the seam allowances toward the triangles. Repeat to make 20 of these units.

Make 20.

3. Sew a red floral triangle to a cream triangle with their short edges aligned and the red triangle on top. Make four units, all with the cream triangle on the left. Press two units with the seam allowances toward the red triangle. Press the other two units with the seam allowances toward the cream triangle.

Make 2. Make 2.

Pieced and quilted by Sue Abrey

4. Using two units from step 3 that have seam allowances pressed toward the red triangle, sew the triangle units to opposite sides of a unit from step 2. Press the seam allowances toward the triangle units.

5. Sew the remaining two triangle units to the other sides of the unit as shown and press the seam allowances toward the triangle units.

6. Repeat steps 3–5 to make a total of 20 blocks.

Make 20.

Assembling the Quilt Top

When laying out your blocks, rotate them as needed to create opposing seams. This will make matching the seam intersections easier.

1. Lay out the blocks in five rows of four blocks each. Sew the blocks together in rows. Press the seam allowances in opposite directions from row to row. Sew the rows together and press all the seam allowances in one direction.

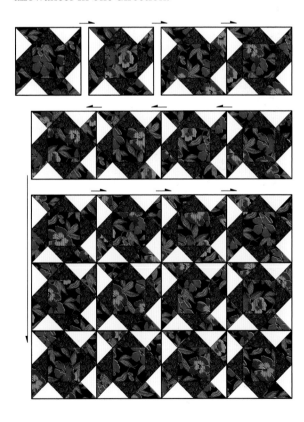

2. Referring to "Making Continuous Strips" on page 10, sew the 1½"-wide black strips together end to end to make a long strip. Referring to "Adding Borders" on page 10, measure, cut, and sew the black strips to the quilt top for the inner border. Press the seam allowances toward the border.

3. Sew the 5½"-wide red floral strips together end to end to make a long strip. Then measure, cut, and sew the red strips to the quilt top for the outer border. Press the seam allowances toward the outer border.

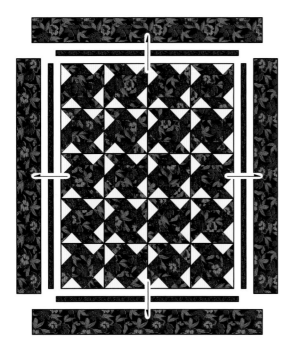

Finishing the Quilt

1. Referring to "Layering and Basting Your Quilt" on page 11, layer the quilt top with batting and backing; baste the layers together. Hand or machine quilt as desired. I used a quilting pattern from Munnich Design. For quilting ideas, refer to "Quilting Option" at right.

2. Using the 2½"-wide black strips, make and attach binding, referring to "Binding Your Quilt" on page 12 as needed.

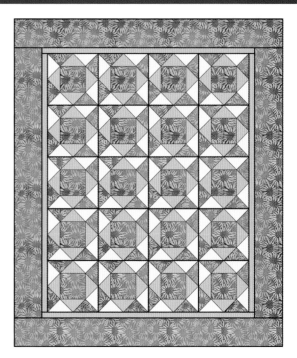

Bring on the cheer with an orange print,
a tan solid, and simple white fabric.

Here's a good example of why you should take your time deciding on a quilting design. I had always intended to use a fairly intricate motif in each block, but when I laid out the quilt and kept looking at it, I thought it would be a shame to lose the secondary pattern where four blocks meet. Instead, I decided to use a fairly loose, edge-to-edge stylized flower, which is one of my favorite quilting designs; that way I wouldn't obscure the secondary pattern.

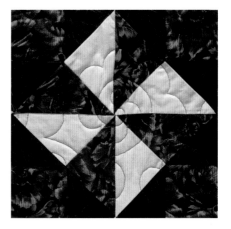

Quilting design copyright is owned by Munnich Design, is used with permission, and may not be copied without the permission of the artist.

◆ Antique Nine Patches ◆

This quilt design is reminiscent of old-fashioned quilt patterns, so I chose to make it in a group of fabrics that reminded me of late Victorian fabric designs and colors.

Quilt size: 52" x 69½"
Block size: 8½" x 8½"
Skill level: Advanced

Materials

Yardage is based on 42"-wide fabric.

- 2⅞ yards of dark red fabric for blocks, sashing, inner border, outer border, and binding
- 1⅜ yards of cream fabric for blocks and middle border
- ½ yard of green fabric for blocks
- ⅝ yard of tan fabric for blocks
- 3½ yards of fabric for backing
- 56" x 74" piece of batting
- Spray starch

Cutting

Since you'll be cutting the cream squares along the bias edge, I recommend that you apply spray starch to these fabrics and press with a dry iron rather than steam before cutting.

From the green fabric, cut:
- 6 strips, 2½" x 42"

From the tan fabric, cut:
- 7 strips, 2½" x 42"

From the dark red fabric, cut:
- 14 strips, 4½" x 42"
- 9 strips, 2½" x 42"

From the cream fabric, cut:
- 6 strips, 6" x 42"; crosscut into 36 squares, 6" x 6". Cut each square in half diagonally to yield 72 triangles.
- 6 strips, 1½" x 42"

Making the Blocks

1. With right sides together, join one green strip and one tan strip along one long edge as shown to make a strip set. Open the strips and press the seam allowances toward the green strip.

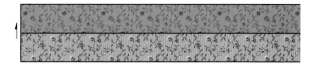

2. In the same manner, sew a second green strip to the tan side of the strip set from step 1 to complete the strip set. Press the seam allowances toward the green strip. Make three strip sets. From the strip sets, cut 36 segments, 2½" wide.

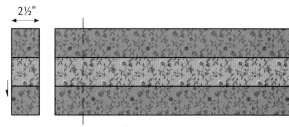

2½"

Make 3 strip sets.
Cut 36 segments.

3. Repeat steps 1 and 2 using one 2½"-wide dark red strip and two tan strips to make a strip set as shown. Press the seam allowances toward the dark red strip. Make two strip sets and cut them into 18 segments, 2½" wide.

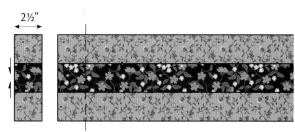

2½"

Make 2 strip sets.
Cut 18 segments.

Pieced and quilted by Sue Abrey

4. Lay out two segments from step 2 and one segment from step 3 as shown. Sew the segments together and press the seam allowances toward the center segment. Repeat to make a total of 18 nine-patch units, each measuring 6½" square.

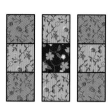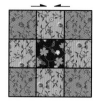

Make 18.

5. Fold a nine-patch unit in half and mark the centers on opposite sides with pins. Fold two cream triangles in half and mark the centers of the long sides with pins. Matching the center pins and with right sides together, sew the triangles to opposite sides of the unit. Press the seam allowances toward the cream triangles. (The triangles were cut oversized and will be trimmed in the next step.)

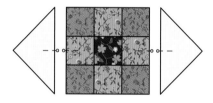

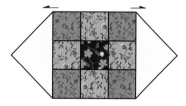

6. In the same manner, center and sew cream triangles to the remaining two sides of the nine-patch unit. Press the seam allowances toward the triangles. Trim and square up the block, making sure to leave ¼" beyond the points of the nine-patch unit for a seam allowance. The block should measure

8½" square. Repeat steps 5 and 6 to make a total of 18 blocks.

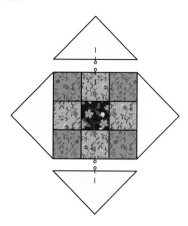

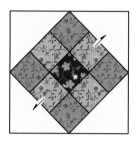

Make 18.

Assembling the Quilt Top

1. Sew the blocks together in three rows of six blocks each. Press the seam allowances open to reduce bulk at the seam intersections.

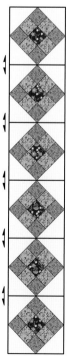

Make 3.

2. Referring to "Making Continuous Strips" on page 10, sew three of the 4½"-wide dark red strips together end to end to make a long strip. Measure the length of each of the three block rows from step 1. If they differ, calculate the average and consider this the length. Cut two strips to that length for your sashing.

3. Lay out the three blocks rows and two sashing strips as shown and sew them together. Press the seam allowances toward the dark red strips. (You'll find it easier if you sew with the block rows on top so you can make sure you're stitching through the seam intersection on each block.)

4. Sew the remaining 4½"-wide dark red strips together end to end to make a long strip, again referring to "Making Continuous Strips" as needed.

5. Sew the 1½"-wide cream strips together end to end to make a long strip.

6. Referring to "Adding Borders" on page 10 and using the long strips from steps 4 and 5, measure, cut, and sew dark red strips to the quilt top for the inner border, cream strips for the middle border, and dark red strips for the outer border. Press all seam allowances toward the outer border.

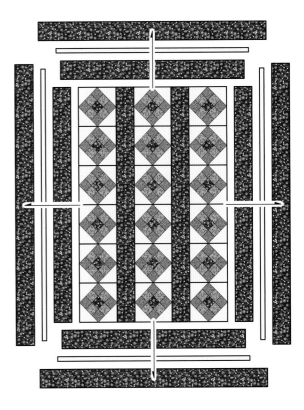

Finishing the Quilt

1. Referring to "Layering and Basting Your Quilt" on page 11, layer the quilt top with batting and backing; baste the layers together. Hand or machine quilt as desired. I used a quilting pattern from Quilters Niche. For quilting ideas, refer to "Quilting Option" on page 72.

2. Using the remaining 2½"-wide dark red strips, make and attach binding, referring to "Binding Your Quilt" on page 12 as needed.

◆ Color Alternatives ◆

For a classic look, choose one each of a dark, medium, and light green print; then set them against a crisp white background.

For a quilt that will remind you of crocus and daffodils, choose dark and light purple fabrics with a multicolored purple print and a little yellow fabric.

◆ Quilting Option ◆

The quilt and its fabrics are very traditional, and I considered quilting feathers in the vertical rows to emphasize the "strippy" effect. However, after looking at the quilt top for a while, I felt that quilted feathers would detract from the fabrics themselves, so I chose a very simple allover quilting design to soften the straight edges of the strips.

Quilting design copyright is owned by Munnich Design, is used with permission, and may not be copied without the permission of the artist.

◆ Lis's Midnight Flower Garden ◆

These are the only type of flowers Lis can work with. She would be the first one to tell you that she can't even keep plastic flowers alive! The black background in this quilt makes the colors really stand out.

Quilt size: 67½" x 80½"
Block size: 12" x 12"
Skill level: Advanced

Materials

Yardage is based on 42"-wide fabric.

- 3¼ yards of black fabric for blocks, sashing, middle border, and binding
- 3⅛ yards of bright pink fabric for blocks, sashing squares, inner border, and outer border
- 1¼ yards of pink floral for blocks
- ⅞ yard of lilac fabric for blocks
- 5 yards of fabric for backing
- 72" x 85" piece of batting

Cutting

From the bright pink fabric, cut:

- 8 strips, 4½" x 42"
- 14 strips, 3" x 42"; crosscut into 180 squares, 3" x 3"
- 7 strips, 2½" x 42"
- 2 strips, 1½" x 42"; crosscut into 30 squares, 1½" x 1½"

From the black fabric, cut:

- 16 strips, 3" x 42"; crosscut into 200 squares, 3" x 3"
- 8 strips, 2½" x 42"
- 24 strips, 1½" x 42"; crosscut *17 of the strips* into 49 strips, 1½" x 12½"

From the lilac fabric, cut:

- 8 strips, 3" x 42"; crosscut into 100 squares, 3" x 3"

From the pink floral, cut:

- 15 strips, 2½" x 42"; crosscut into 240 squares, 2½" x 2½"

Making the Blocks

1. Draw a diagonal line from corner to corner on the wrong side of each 3" bright pink square. Layer a marked bright pink square right sides together with 140 black squares and stitch ¼" from each side of the marked line. Cut the squares apart on the drawn line. Press the seam allowances toward the bright pink triangles. Trim each unit to measure 2½" square. Make 280 half-square-triangle units.

Make 280.

2. Repeat step 1, sewing the remaining bright pink squares right sides together with 40 lilac squares to make half-square-triangle units. Press the seam allowances toward the bright pink triangles and trim. Make 80 units.

Make 80.

3. Draw a diagonal line from corner to corner on the wrong side of each remaining lilac square. In the same manner as step 1, layer marked lilac squares right sides together with black squares. Stitch and then cut the squares apart to make half-square-triangle units. Press the seam allowances toward the black triangles and trim. Make 120 of these units.

Make 120.

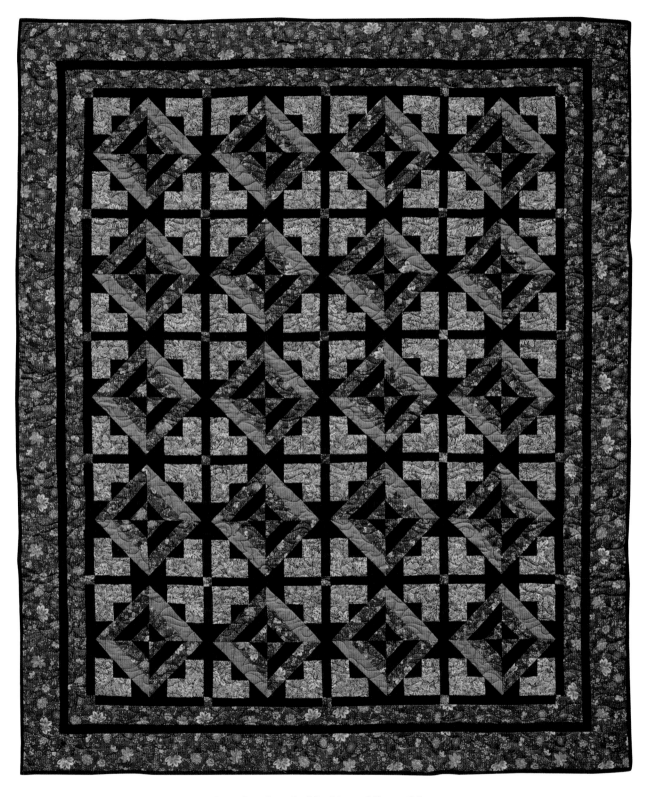

Pieced and quilted by Lis and Drew Moore

4. Lay out 14 units from step 1, four units from step 2, six units from step 3, and 12 pink floral squares in six rows as shown. Sew the pieces into rows, pressing the seam allowances in opposite directions from row to row. Sew the rows together and press the seam allowances as shown. The block should measure 12½" square. Repeat to make a total of 20 blocks.

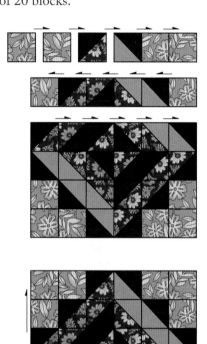

Make 20.

Assembling the Quilt Top

1. Sew together four 1½" x 12½" black sashing strips and five 1½" bright pink squares to make a sashing row, alternating them as shown. Press the seam allowances toward the sashing strips. Repeat to make a total of six rows.

Make 6.

2. Sew together four blocks and five 1½" x 12½" black sashing strips to make a block row, alternating them as shown. Press the seam allowances toward the sashing strips. Repeat to make a total of five rows.

Make 5.

3. Sew the block rows and sashing rows together; press all seam allowances toward the sashing rows.

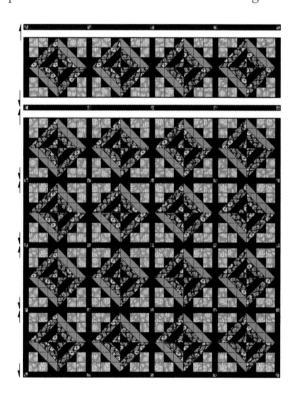

4. Referring to "Making Continuous Strips" on page 10, sew the 2½"-wide bright pink strips together end to end to make a long strip. Referring to "Adding Borders" on page 10, measure, cut, and sew the bright pink strips to the quilt top for the inner border. Press the seam allowances toward the border.

5. Repeat step 4 using the remaining 1½"-wide black strips for the middle border and the 4½"-wide bright pink strips for the outer border. Press the seam allowances toward the outer border.

Finishing the Quilt

1. Referring to "Layering and Basting Your Quilt" on page 11, layer the quilt top with batting and backing; baste the layers together. Hand or machine quilt as desired. For quilting ideas, refer to "Quilting Option" at right.
2. Using the 2½"-wide black strips, make and attach binding, referring to "Binding Your Quilt" on page 12 as needed.

◆ Color Alternative ◆

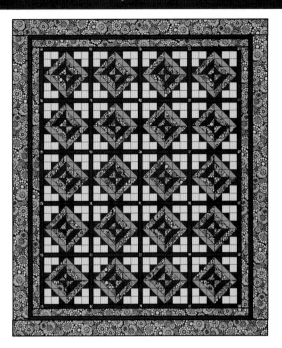

Transform the "Midnight Flower Garden" into a daytime oasis by combining neutral browns and tans with shots of coral and a multicolored floral.

◆ Quilting Option ◆

The fabrics and blocks make this quilt look busy. The original intention was to quilt a motif in each block, and then something different in the sashing and borders. On reflection though, Lis realized that most of the quilting would be lost in the blocks, so she chose an allover quilting design, which, in places, echoed the shape of the flowers in the fabrics.

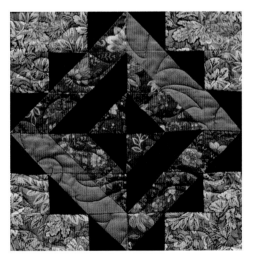

Quilting design copyright is owned by Munnich Design, is used with permission, and may not be copied without the permission of the artist.

◆ Suppliers ◆

Fabrics

Fabric Freedom
www.fabricfreedom.co.uk

Digital Quilting Designs

The following websites offer down-loadable quilting patterns. Preprinted patterns may also be available.

Munnich Design
www.quiltrecipes.com

Quilters Niche
www.quiltersniche.com

Digi Tech
www.digitechpatterns.com

Intelligent Quilting
www.intelligentquilting.com

◆ Acknowledgments ◆

There are some people I particularly want to thank for their support while I was writing this book.

First, thanks go to Kim Brackett: you've been a wonderful mentor to me during this whole process and I would never have been able to do it without you.

Lis and Drew, who made some of the quilts in this book for me and acted as great pattern testers. I can't tell you how grateful I am to you both for your help, which made such a difference to me.

Roberta, who also tested patterns for me: I'm thankful for your willing and fast assistance even though you weren't in the best of health at the time.

Martingale & Company: you also deserve my thanks for your speedy and ever-cheerful responses to all my questions, no matter how stupid you must have thought me at times.

Since I'm British, it seemed right to use British fabrics wherever possible for the quilts in this book, so I want to say thank you to Fabric Freedom, a British manufacturing company, for kindly letting me loose in your warehouse and donating all the fabrics and the batting (wadding) that I wanted. Thank you.

I can't finish without also saying thanks to Helen, Jayne, Ali, and Kathy, who believed in me, even when I didn't; to my father, who patiently sat and listened to me moaning when things seemed to be going wrong; and, finally to my family, for their love and support always.

◆ About the Author ◆

I'm a wife, mother, grandmother, daughter, sister, and quilter. I was born in London (although I'm not quite a cockney) and spent most of my life in the south of England. Ten years ago my husband and I moved "oop north" and took early retirement. I now live and quilt in West Yorkshire.

When I learned needlework at school, I hated it, and I don't think I ever finished my first project, an apron! My love of quilting started about 12 years ago when, one day, I walked past a quilt shop and was stopped in my tracks by a quilt in the window. Of course, I had to go in to have a closer look, and the rest, as they say, is history.

Since that day I've made many quilts, usually to my own design. My quilts are traditional pieced quilts, and I love to hand quilt, although it's very time-consuming. I'm now lucky enough to have a computerized, long-arm quilting system, which gives me time to design and make even more quilts.

◆ There's More Online! ◆

See blogs about her quilting life and more at http://quilttimes.blogspot.com.

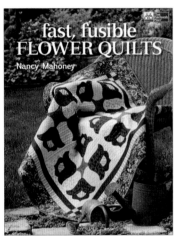
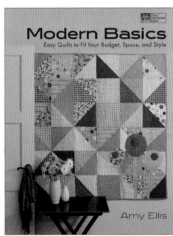

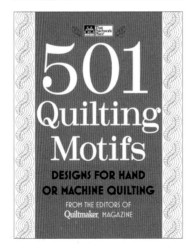